Victoria E. Henderson

WHEN I NEED A WORD, GOD SPEAKS! Journal

Studio Griffin
A Publishing Company
www.studiogriffin.net

For information, contact:
Studio Griffin
A Publishing Company
Garner, North Carolina
studiogriffin@outlook.com
www.studiogriffin.net

Cover Design by Ruth E. Griffin
Photo by © Victoria E. Henderson

Scripture quotations marked KJV taken from The Holy Bible, King James Version. New York: American Bible Society: 1999.

Scripture quotations marked NIV taken from the Holy Bible, New International Version®. Copyright © 1973, 1978, 1984 International Bible Society. Used by permission of Zondervan. All rights reserved. The "NIV" and "New International Version" trademarks are registered in the United States Patent and Trademark Office by International Bible Society. Use of either trademark requires the permission of International Bible Society.

Scripture quotations marked Message taken from The Message: The Bible in Contemporary Language. Peterson, Eugene H. Colorado Springs: NavPress, 2002. Print.

Scripture quotations marked NKJV taken from The Holy Bible: New King James Version. Holman Bible Publishers, 2013.

Scripture quotations marked GNT taken from Holy Bible: The Good News Translation (2nd ed). 1992. New York: American Bible Society.

First Edition

ISBN: 978-1-954818-26-2

Library of Congress Control Number: 2021951129

1 2 3 4 5 6 7 8 9 10

MY TESTIMONY

I contracted COVID-19 in early 2021 and, for three weeks, this was a very traumatic period. I had a temperature I could not shake for seven days and a terrible cough. The truth was, I did not think I was going to make it, especially hearing the number of COVID-19 deaths broadcast daily. I lost friends and acquaintances to COVID-19 during the same time I was sick. I had to turn off the television and focus on healing.

I am forever grateful to those praying friends of mine who would not let me forget that I was loved, and that God was a Healer. I listened to sermons, gospel music and prayed as much as my addled brain could. Some days, all I could say was, "Jesus, Jesus!" And that was all I needed to say. I called on His Name, and He heard my cry. Glory be to my Lord and Savior, Jesus Christ, for loving me beyond my comprehension, saving my life, and giving me a new purpose.

TABLE OF CONTENTS

INTRODUCTION

Have you ever wondered if God was really speaking to you? Have you thought you heard His voice, but you were not sure if it was Him or not? Maybe you thought, "God surely would not speak to little old me!" That is exactly what I thought until I learned to take the time to hear God in every area of my life. God would use simple concepts and sometimes complex situations to get me to see the lessons He prepared for me.

When I started this journal, it was my intention to guide you on a path to be able to hear God speak. As I went along, it became clear that this would also be a time for you to reflect on your own life and work towards healing in some areas. To be honest, it is doing that for me as well.

My prayer is that God will reveal Himself to you in ways never thought of as you take the time to meet with Him! Thank you for being willing to go on this faith journey! The best is yet to come! May God bless you as you seek to hear His voice.

About The Journal

I have shared how God speaks to me in my book, When I Need A Word, God Speaks! This companion journal is designed for you to take a few steps to learn how God speaks to you! You will need the book in order to walk through the journal. I have referenced the pages you need in each section.

The journal takes the book and divides it into sections five days at a time, so that you can take time to contemplate the lessons and apply them to your life. Days Six and Seven are devoted to going back and reviewing just how God showed up as you waited to hear from Him. It is on those pages of reflection that I pray you find healing from old wounds and the courage to trust God. This is your personal journal. Use it to be honest with yourself and remember—there is no right or wrong way to answer. This is your life! You have to do the work to see results. Let's go!

WEEK ONE

DAY ONE
For I Know The Plans

Jeremiah 29:11: For I know the thoughts that I think toward you, saith the LORD, thoughts of peace and not of evil, to give you an expected end. (KJV).

What are your first thoughts after reading this passage from pages 3-5 in the book? Do you believe God has plans for you?

Application to My Life

Is there anything you have been impressed to do that you have put off? What would be the first steps to make it happen?

____

____

____

____

____

____

____

____

Prayer Time

Dear God, help me to spend time listening for Your voice. Help me to discover my calling and purpose. I know that it is not too late! I know that You know the plan for my life. I trust You to bring to completion the good works You have begun in me. Amen.

My Prayers and Praises

____

____

____

____

____

____

____

____

DAY TWO
I Need To Eat

Matthew 4:4: Jesus answered, "It is written: 'Man shall not live on bread alone, but on every word that comes from the mouth of God. (NIV)

What are your first thoughts after reading this passage from pages 6-8 in the book? Do you feel yourself needing to be in God's presence?

____

____

____

____

____

____

____

____

____

____

____

____

____

____

____

____

____

____

____

____

Application To My Life

Do you feel that belonging to a church or place of worship is important to you? Why or why not?

____

____

____

____

____

____

____

____

Prayer Time

Dear God, help me spend more time in Your presence so that I can know You for myself. I ask You for the courage to always walk in Your purpose for me. I need to eat indeed. Amen.

My Prayers and Praises

____

____

____

____

____

____

____

____

DAY THREE
What's So Good About It?

Psalms 69:34: You heavens, praise him; praise him, earth; Also ocean and all things that swim in it. (Message)

What are your first thoughts after reading this passage from pages 9-13 in the book? How do you handle not-so-good days?

____

____

____

____

____

____

____

____

____

____

____

____

____

____

____

____

____

____

Application To My Life

Can you recall a time when your heart was bursting with praise? How did that make you feel? Did you think God was speaking to you?

____

____

____

____

____

____

____

____

____

Prayer Time

Dear God, I thank You today for being so good to me. I praise You for the many ways You show Your love for me, and I am grateful. You are indeed a good God! Amen.

My Prayers and Praises

____

____

____

____

____

____

____

____

____

DAY FOUR
Because He Loves Me

Isaiah 43:1-4: But now, God's Message, the God who made you in the first place, Jacob, the One who got you started, Israel: "Don't be afraid, I've redeemed you. I've called your name. You're mine. When you're in over your head, I'll be there with you. When you're in rough waters, you will not go down. When you're between a rock and a hard place, it won't be a dead end— Because I am God, your personal God, The Holy of Israel, your Savior. I paid a huge price for you: all of Egypt, with rich Cush and Seba thrown in! That's how much you mean to me! That's how much I love you! I'd sell off the whole world to get you back, trade the creation just for you. (Message)

What are your first thoughts after reading this passage from pages 11-13 in the book? Do you feel that God loves you?

____

____

____

____

____

____

____

____

____

____

____

____

____

____

____

____

Application To My Life

Has there been a time in your life when you felt alone? That God was far away? How did you overcome the feelings?

____

____

____

____

____

____

____

____

Prayer Time

Dear God, there are times when life overwhelms me. I get tired and frustrated. I thank You for showing me that You love me and will never leave me alone, even in small ways. Thank You for taking good care of me. Amen.

My Prayers and Praises

____

____

____

____

____

____

____

____

DAY FIVE
Today I Cried

Psalm 56:8-9: Thou tellest my wanderings: put thou my tears into thy bottle: are they not in thy book? When I cry unto thee, then shall mine enemies turn back: this I know; for God is for me. (KJV)

What are your first thoughts after reading this passage from pages 14-18 in the book? Do you think of tears differently?

____

____

____

____

____

____

____

____

____

____

____

____

____

____

____

____

____

____

Application To My Life

Are you a person who cries easily? Do you cry around others? Do you think tears have a purpose?

____

____

____

____

____

____

____

____

____

Prayer Time

Dear God, help me to remember Your promise that all my tears will be wiped away forever! Thank You for seeing my pain and knowing what my heart cannot express in words. Amen.

My Prayers and Praises

____

____

____

____

____

____

____

____

WEEK ONE LESSONS

Take some time to review your life applications and reflections over the past week. What did God speak to you? How were you more aware of His presence this week?

Lord, I thank You for being with me this past week. Help me to be open to hearing You in new ways. Thank You for being with me. Amen.

My Prayer and Praises

____

____

____

____

____

____

____

____

____

____

WEEK TWO

DAY ONE
Inside The Fish

Jonah 2 1-2: From inside the fish Jonah prayed to the LORD his God. He said: "In my distress I called to the LORD, and he answered me. From the depths of the grave, I called for help, and you listened to my cry. (NIV)

What are your first thoughts after reading this passage from pages 19-21 in the book? Do you think you could praise inside a nasty fish?

Application To My Life

Can you recall a time in your life when you had to praise through a situation? Did you feel stronger after that experience?

____

____

____

____

____

____

____

____

____

Prayer Time

Dear God, there are times when it is difficult to praise when I am hurting or going through something. Help me to praise anyway while I trust You to bring me out. Amen.

My Prayers and Praises

____

____

____

____

____

____

____

____

DAY TWO
Outside the Fish

Jonah 4:1-2: But it displeased Jonah exceedingly, and he became angry. So, he prayed to the Lord, and said, "Ah, Lord, was not this what I said when I was still in my country? (KJV)

What are your first thoughts after reading this passage from pages 22-24 in the book? Have you ever felt like Jonah?

Application To My Life

Do you feel God speaking to you in big or small ways yet?

____

____

____

____

____

____

____

____

____

Prayer Time

Dear Lord, help me to be a witness to everyone I meet and to remember the love and mercy You showed me must be extended to all. Amen.

My Prayers and Praises

____

____

____

____

____

____

____

____

____

DAY THREE
The Perfume of My Life

Proverbs 27:9: Ointment and perfume rejoice the heart: so doth the sweetness of a man's friend by hearty counsel. (KJV)

What are your first thoughts after reading this passage from pages 25-38 in the book? Do you think we need only to use certain things on special occasions?

Application To My Life

What could you be holding on to that you need to let go of?

____

____

____

____

____

____

____

____

____

Prayer Time

Dear Lord, help me to not let material things be my focus from day to day. Help me to let the light of Your love shine in me everywhere I go. Amen.

My Prayers and Praises

____

____

____

____

____

____

____

____

DAY FOUR
It's A Process

*Exodus 2:23: And it came to pass in **process** of time... (KJV)*

*Judges 11:4: And it came to pass in **process** of time...(KJV)*

*2 Chronicles 21:19: And it came to pass, that in **process** of time... (KJV)*

What are your first thoughts after reading this passage from pages 28-31 in the book? What does "the process" mean to you?

____

____

____

____

____

____

____

____

____

____

____

____

____

____

____

____

Application To My Life

How have you handled the processes in your life? How has God shown Himself to you during those times?

____

____

____

____

____

____

____

____

____

____

Prayer Time

Dear Lord, help me to remember that You are always with me no matter the situation. Thank You for Your love. Amen.

My Prayers and Praises

____

____

____

____

____

____

____

____

____

DAY FIVE
The Red Sea Experience

Exodus 15:21, 22: And Moses stretched out his hand over the sea; and the LORD caused the sea to go back by a strong east wind all that night, and made the sea dry land, and the waters were divided. And the children of Israel went into the midst of the sea upon the dry ground: and the waters were a wall unto them on their right hand, and on their left. (KJV)

What are your first thoughts after reading this passage from pages 32-35 in the book? Can you imagine how the Israelites must have felt seeing that water divide?

____

____

____

____

Application To My Life

Can you recall a time when you truly didn't know what to do or which way to go? How did God speak to you and guide you during the situation?

____

____

____

____

____

____

____

____

____

Prayer Time

Dear Lord, there are times when I just don't know what to do or which way to go. I want to trust that it will all work out, but I get scared. Help me to remember to lean on You. Amen.

My Prayers and Praises

____

____

____

____

____

____

____

____

WEEK TWO LESSONS

Take some time to review your life applications and reflections over the past week. What did God speak to you? How were you more aware of His presence this week?

Prayer Time

Lord, I thank You for being with me this past week. Help me to be open to hearing You in new ways. Thank You for being with me. Amen.

My Prayer and Praises

____

____

____

____

____

____

____

____

____

____

WEEK THREE

DAY ONE
I Choose To Worship

2 Samuel 12: 19-21: But when David saw that his servants whispered, David perceived that the child was dead. Therefore, David said unto his servants, "Is the child dead?" And they said, "He is dead." [20] Then David arose from the earth, and washed and anointed himself and changed his apparel, and came into the house of the Lord, and worshiped. Then he came to his own house; and when he required, they set bread before him and he ate. [21] Then said his servants unto him, "What thing is this that thou hast done? Thou did fast and weep for the child while it was alive, but when the child was dead, thou did rise and eat bread." (KJV)

After reading about David from this passage on pages 36-38 in the book, what are your first thoughts?

____

____

____

____

____

____

____

____

____

____

____

____

____

____

____

____

____

Application To My Life

Do you find it difficult to worship when going through a storm in your life?

____

____

____

____

____

____

____

____

Prayer Time

Dear Lord, I want to worship You through the good and the bad. Help me to keep my trust in You no matter what it looks or feels like. Amen.

My Prayers and Praises

____

____

____

____

____

____

____

____

DAY TWO
Wouldn't Take Nothing For My Journey Now!

Philippians 3:13: Brethren, I count not myself to have apprehended: but this one thing I do, forgetting those things which are behind, and reaching forth unto those things which are before. (KJV)

After reading this passage from pages 39-42 in the book, what are your first thoughts about birthdays and grate-fulness?

Application To My Life

What does self-care mean to you? In what ways are you practicing self-care on your journey? What are some ways you can do better?

____

____

____

____

____

____

____

____

____

Prayer Time

Dear Lord, I am grateful indeed for Your love. Please walk with me on my journey and help me take better care of myself along the way. Amen.

My Prayers and Praises

____

____

____

____

____

____

____

____

____

DAY THREE
The Voice

John 10:27: My sheep hear my voice, and I know them, and they follow me: (KJV)

What are your first thoughts after reading this passage from pages 43-45 in the book? Do you hear God's voice directing you? In what way?

Application To My Life

How can you weed out the noise in your life to be able to hear God more?

____

____

____

____

____

____

____

____

____

____

Prayer Time

Dear Lord, there are times when I am not sure if the voice I hear is Yours. Help me to be still and listen and look for You in everything I do. Amen.

My Prayers and Praises

____

____

____

____

____

____

____

____

DAY FOUR
Lord, Fix My Life!

Psalm 51:7: Purge me with hyssop, and I shall be clean: wash me, and I shall be whiter than snow. (KJV)

What are your first thoughts after reading this passage from pages 46-49 in the book? Is there anyone you respect, like Iyanla Vanzant?

Application To My Life

Have you tried to fix certain areas of your life on your own? How has that worked out or not?

____

____

____

____

____

____

____

____

Prayer Time

Dear Lord, there are some things in me that I know only You can fix. Help me to lean on You and get professional help if I need it too. Amen.

My Prayers and Praises

____

____

____

____

____

____

____

____

____

DAY FIVE
A Scandal Only God Can Handle

Philippians 4:8: In conclusion, my friends, fill your minds with those things that are good and that deserve praise: things that are true, noble, right, pure, lovely, and honorable. (GNT)

What are your first thoughts after reading this passage from pages 50-53 in the book? Do you think some television shows are really all that bad?

____

____

____

____

____

____

____

____

____

____

____

____

____

____

____

____

____

____

____

Application To My Life

Are there some shows that you love that you know may not be the best for you? Are you willing to try and not watch for a bit?

____

____

____

____

____

____

____

____

____

Prayer Time

Dear Lord, if I am honest, I have had a few scandals too. Forgive my past as I walk in a new way of life. Amen.

My Prayers and Praises

____

____

____

____

____

____

____

____

WEEK THREE LESSONS

Take some time to review your life applications and reflections over the past week. What did God speak to you? How were you more aware of His presence this week? Did you take the time to speak back?

Prayer Time

Lord, I thank You for being with me this past week. Help me to be open to hearing You in new ways. Thank You for being with me. Amen.

My Prayer and Praises

____

____

____

____

____

____

____

____

____

____

WEEK FOUR

DAY ONE
I See ME

2 Corinthians 3:18 But we all, with unveiled face, beholding as in a mirror the glory of the Lord, are being transformed into the same image from glory to glory, just as by the Spirit of the Lord. (NKJV)

What are your first thoughts after reading this passage from pages 54-58 in the book? Do you need to take better care of you?

Application To My Life

How do you really see yourself at this moment? Is your view positive or negative?

____

____

____

____

____

____

____

____

Prayer Time

Dear Lord, let me see myself as worthy because You gave Your very life for me. Amen.

My Prayers and Praises

Find some verses in the Bible that talk about how much God loves you! Put your name in them and make them personal! List them below.

____

____

____

____

____

____

____

____

____

DAY TWO
Love Is An Action Word

I John 3:16-17: This is how we've come to understand and experience love: Christ sacrificed his life for us. This is why we ought to live sacrificially for our fellow believers, and not just be out for ourselves. If you see some brother or sister in need and have the means to do something about it but turn a cold shoulder and do nothing, what happens to God's love? It disappears. And you made it disappear. (Message)

What are your first thoughts after reading this passage from pages 59-63 in the book? What does love in action mean to you?

____

____

____

____

____

____

____

____

____

____

____

____

____

____

____

____

Application To My Life

When you look at how people have hurt you (children or otherwise), how were you able to process through it?

____

____

____

____

____

____

____

____

Prayer Time

Pray what is in your heart over regret, and if you have children, what you want the Lord to do.

My Prayers and Praises

Further Food for Thought: Think of a time when you were really hurt. How are you able to forgive? Was it hard to extend grace toward them?

____

____

____

____

____

____

____

____

DAY THREE
Orange Juice Praise

1 Peter 1:7: That the trial of your faith, being much more precious than of gold that perisheth, though it be tried with fire, might be found unto praise and honour and glory at the appearing of Jesus Christ. (KJV)

What are your first thoughts after reading this passage from pages 64-68 of the book? Can you believe all that came from spilling orange juice?

____

____

____

____

____

____

____

____

____

____

____

____

____

____

____

____

____

____

____

Application To My Life

Can you describe a time in your life when one thing happened that led you to a deeper discovery?

____

____

____

____

____

____

____

____

____

Prayer Time

Lord, help me to see that there may be deeper lessons I need to learn when something happens unexpectedly. Amen.

My Prayers and Praises

Further Food for Thought: Do you wear masks at time to cover your real feelings? What are ways you think God can help you in this area? Take time to talk with God now about your masks.

____

____

____

____

____

____

____

____

DAY FOUR
A Temporary Inconvenience!

2 Corinthians 1:17: That as ye are partakers of the sufferings, so shall ye be also of the consolation. (KJV)

What are your first thoughts after reading this passage from pages 69-72 in the book? How have you reacted when you are inconvenienced?

Have you looked at inconveniences in your life as temporary and life lessons? If not, why not?

____

____

____

____

____

Prayer Time

Lord, I can get frustrated when things happen. Help me to think clearly during those times and cast my burdens on You. Amen.

Further Food for Thought

Spend the next fifteen minutes in prayer. Talk to God about anything on your heart. Speak openly about your feelings if you are going through something and need God to move on your behalf. Praise Him for being with you!

____

____

____

____

____

My Prayers and Praises

____

____

____

____

____

WEEK FOUR LESSONS

Take some time to review your life applications and reflections over the past week. What did God speak to you? How were you more aware of His presence this week? Did you take the time to speak back?

Lord, I thank You for being with me this past week. Help me to be open to hearing You in new ways. Thank You for being with me. Amen.

My Prayer and Praises

WEEK FIVE

Moving Forward

The last three chapters of the book are about courage and starting again with God. Use these lessons to draw closer to God and renew your commitment to deepening your relationship with Him. There are further 'Food For Thought' reflections in this section.

DAY ONE
Courage Not To Quit

Joshua 1:9: Be strong and of a good courage; be not afraid, neither be thou dismayed: for the Lord thy God is with thee whithersoever thou goest. (KJV)

What are your first thoughts after reading this passage from pages 73-75 in the book? What does courage mean to you?

Application To My Life

Was there a time in your life when you had to muster more courage than you thought you had? What was that like for you?

____

____

____

____

____

____

Prayer Time

Lord, help me to have courage not to quit when life gets hard. I love You, and I trust You. Amen.

Further Food for Thought

Look up the definition of 'courage.' Write it here. Ask God to give you the courage that endures all things. Praise Him for having it even when it did not feel like you did.

____

____

____

____

____

My Prayers and Praises

____

____

____

____

DAY TWO
Back to Basics

Hebrews 11:6: But without faith it is impossible to please Him, for he who comes to God must believe that He is, and that He is a rewarder of those who diligently seek Him. (NKJV)

What are your first thoughts after reading this passage from pages 76-78 in the book? Is your first response to pray as soon as something happens, good or bad?

____

____

____

____

____

____

____

____

____

____

____

____

____

____

____

____

____

____

Application To My Life

Do you find it hard to 'let go and let God' have control in every area of your life?

____

____

____

____

____

____

Prayer Time

Lord, help me to truly trust in You to direct me in every area of my life. Amen.

Further Food for Thought

Describe what going back to basics with God means to you. What changes will you make to spend more time with Him?

____

____

____

____

____

____

My Prayers and Praises

____

____

____

____

DAY THREE
A Year in the Life

Psalm 102:27: But thou are the same, and they years shall have not end. (NKJV)

What are your first thoughts after reading this passage from pages 79-83 in the book? Have you ever felt stuck, so to speak?

____

____

____

____

____

____

____

____

____

____

____

____

____

____

____

____

____

____

____

Application To My Life

Can you identify something you just know you should be doing but have not yet? What are some of the barriers preventing you from doing it?

____

____

____

____

____

____

Prayer Time

Lord, please help me to be patient with myself. Direct me in the way I should go so I can always do what I need to do for You. Amen.

Further Food for Thought

Procrastination can stop you from reaching for everything God has for you. Can you identify one or two things you need to do and write down the steps you need to take to get them done? Praise God for the finished work!

____

____

____

____

____

My Prayers and Praises

____

____

____

____

WEEK FIVE LESSONS

Take some time to review your life applications and reflections over the past week. What did God speak to you? How were you more aware of His presence this week?

Prayer Time

Lord, I thank You for being with me this past week. Help me to be open to hearing You in new ways. Thank You for being with me. Amen.

My Prayer and Praises

FINAL THOUGHTS

Take some time to review your weekly lessons, life applications, reflections, prayers, and praises in the coming days. I pray that God has spoken to you, and you know without a doubt that it is Him! When I began my walk with Him and truly opened my heart, I found that He spoke to me in ways that were designed just for me. While working on this journal, God used it as another vehicle for me to hear what was uniquely for me. I learned to take the time to be quiet and listen for what He was telling me in the stillness. As the questions came in response to the readings, I was required to answer them as well and found there were places I needed healing in.

Whatever lessons you learned through this journal, and in whatever ways God spoke to you and healed your soul, my prayer is that you walk in victory from this day forward. Share your story with someone else and help them heal too. The beautiful part of all this is that the journey is not over. We learn daily about the depth of God's never-ending love for us. Never stop listening for ways to hear God. Then, do what He says do. You will never regret it!

ACKNOWLEDGEMENTS

This project would not be complete without my YES, SISTERS who told me I could do it, reminded me it was time to get back to it, and gently pushed me when procrastination tried to rear its ugly head. I am here because of your unending love, prayers, and support.

Chanelle L. Henderson, Ruth E. Griffin, Andrea L. Hines, Beghetta L. Liles, and Lori E. Livingstone—this one's for you! Thank you is simply not enough. I love you all!

ABOUT THE AUTHOR

Victoria E. Henderson was born and raised in New York City, where she cultivated her love for reading and writing stories. This passion turned into messages of love and hope for her friends, who encouraged her to start her blog, "Still Waters."

Victoria knows firsthand what juggling truly means. Along with family responsibilities, Victoria serves as a Budget Analyst at a large public school district. She earned her BA in Psychology from North Carolina Central University in December of 2012 and has taken quite a few classes in pursuit of her master's in counseling.

Victoria is also a co-host on a live internet radio show with author friends, Andrea L. Hines, and Ruth E. Griffin, called Authors Up, which showcases other authors' work during interviews. The show encourages everyone in their writing with tips, timely information, and inspiration for the journey. In keeping with her encouraging spirit, Victoria posted weekly videos on Facebook and Instagram by sharing testimonies and songs that echoes her motto – "If I can help somebody, then my living shall not be in vain". She has now turned that into a live show which airs the second and fourth Mondays of each month called "Living Life Victoriously". Both shows can be seen on ALH Broadcasting on Facebook and at Streaming Inspirational Broadcasting Network on YouTube.

Victoria owns her own business called Victoria's Treasure Box. She sells beautiful and affordable Paparazzi jewelry to her customers who she calls Treasureville. She inspires and encourages all to be their best selves inside and out.

Victoria's first book, When I Need a Word, God Speaks! was released on July 31, 2019. The accompanying journal was released in September 2021. You can get copies on Amazon, Barnes & Noble, or wherever books are sold. Check out her blog at www.victoriaehenderson.com where you can sign up and receive email notification when the new ones hit.

Victoria resides in North Carolina where she enjoys spending time with her family, watching her children become who they want to be, and especially, worshipping God in all circumstances.